Contents

Words in bold are in the glossary on page 23.

Welcome to Poland

Hello! I live in Poland. Witam is the Polish word for welcome. Polish people are very friendly and proud of their country.

Where is Poland?

Poland is a beautiful country in central Europe. It is a bit bigger than the UK. Poland shares **borders** with seven other countries, including Germany, Slovakia, Ukraine and Russia. The northern border runs along the Baltic Sea.

Lithuania

Russia

Baltic Sea

GDAŃSK

Vistula

Belarus

Germany

POLAND

WARSAW

WROCŁAW

ŁÓDŹ

KATOWICE

KRAKÓW

Sudety Mountains

Carpathian Mountains

Tatras Mountains

Ukraine

Czech Republic

Slovakia

N
W E
S

LIVING IN EUROPE

Living in
POLAND

Annabelle Lynch

W

FRANKLIN WATTS
LONDON·SYDNEY

Franklin Watts
First published in 2016 by the Watts Publishing Group

Credits
Series Editor: Julia Bird
Series Design: D.R. ink

ISBN 978 1 4451 4856 4

Picture credits: Africa Studio/Shutterstock: 15t. alicjane/Shutterstock: 12b. Matyas Arval/Shutterstock: 13t. badahos/Shutterstock: 8b, 20b. Tomasz Bidermann/Shutterstock: 17bl. Maciej Bledowski/Shutterstock: 5b, 17t. Igor Boldyrev//Shutterstock: 17c. Bonchan/Shutterstock: 15c. borzywoj/Shutterstock: 10b. Brainsil/Shutterstock: 8t. Djem/Shutterstock: 4t. Milosz-G/Shutterstock: 12c. Agnes Kantaruk/Dreamstime: 11t. Pawel Kazmierczak/Shutterstock: 5t. Christian Kober/Robert Harding PL: 14-15c. Marcin Kryzak/Shutterstock: 6br. Michal Ludwiczak/istockphoto: 14b. Madzia71/istock: 21b. Steven May/Alamy: 9b. m jrn/Shutterstock: 6bl. Guilio Napolitano/Shutterstock: 7t. Nightman1965/Shutterstock: 11b. Pe 3k/Shutterstock: 18b. Pegaz/Alamy: 14t. Photocreo/Michal Bednarek/Shutterstock: 20c. Pressmaster/Shutterstock: 16t. Sanneberg/Shutterstock: 18t. Sepy67/Dreamstime: 10t. S-F/Shutterstock: front cover. Smellme/Dreamstime: 19t. Krystyna Szulecka/Alamy: 17br. Ar Tono/Shutterstock: 19b. De Visu/Shutterstock: 21t. Tatyana Vychegzhanina/Dreamstime: 9t. Ivonne Wierink/Dreamstime: 6t. Marcos Mesa Sam Wordley/Shutterstock: 12t. Anna Yakimova/Dreamstime: 20t. Piotr Zajc/Shutterstock: 16b, 22b. Beata Zawrel/Demotix/Corbis: 7b. Rudmer Zwerver/Shutterstock: 13b.

FSC
www.fsc.org
MIX
Paper from
responsible sources
FSC® C104740

Printed in China

Franklin Watts
An imprint of
Hachette Children's Group
Part of The Watts Publishing Group
Carmelite House
50 Victoria Embankment
London EC4Y 0DZ

An Hachette UK Company
www.hachette.co.uk

www.franklinwatts.co.uk

Plains and mountains

There are high mountains in southern Poland. But most of the country is low-lying **plains**. In fact, the word Poland means 'plains' in the language of a people called the **Slavs**. Most Polish people are **descended from** Slavs who settled in Poland over 1,500 years ago.

Tatra Mountains

Castle Square in Warsaw in summer.

Weather

The weather in Poland changes with the seasons. Spring is usually mild. Summer is warm and rainy. Autumn brings cool, sunny weather. Winters are cold and frosty, with snow in the mountains.

People in Poland

I come from Poland. People from Poland are called Poles.

City and countryside

Over 38 million people live in Poland. Six out of every ten people live in cities. The rest live in the countryside. In cities most people live in tall blocks of flats. In the countryside, many people live in small houses made of brick or wood. Some houses have **thatched** roofs.

On the move

Many young Poles from the countryside move to the cities to find work. Young people also go abroad to get a job in Germany, the UK and other European countries. In turn, people from neighbouring countries such as Ukraine come to Poland to look for work.

Religion

Religion is important in Poland. Most people are Roman Catholics. They go to church to celebrate **mass** on Sundays. Some people follow other Christian religions, such as Protestant or Eastern Orthodox. There are also Jews and Muslims.

Pope John Paul II came from Poland.

Catholic girls celebrate their first Holy Communion.

Warsaw

*I live in Warsaw. Warsaw is the **capital** of Poland. It is also the biggest city, with 1.7 million people.*

Old and new

Warsaw has a mix of old and new buildings. You can see a castle and a palace where Polish kings once lived.

You can also see **parliament** buildings. Warsaw's old town was bombed during the Second World War (1939–1945), but it was rebuilt, and is now as beautiful as ever.

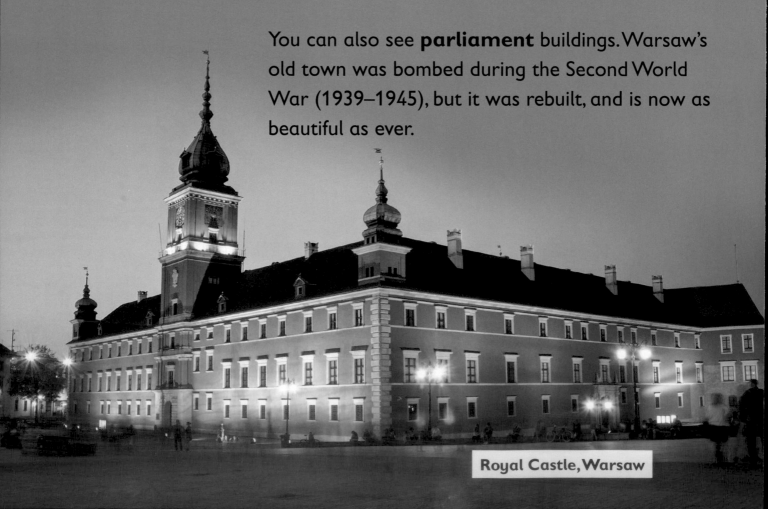

Royal Castle, Warsaw

The Vistula flows through Warsaw.

Poland's longest river

Warsaw lies on the Vistula. This long river begins in the mountains in southern Poland, and winds right across the country to the Baltic Sea.

Work and travel

In Warsaw people work in shops, cafés, hotels, offices and factories. Other people work as teachers, doctors, nurses or bus and tram drivers. People get to work by tram, bus or the metro. Some people travel by bike, motorbike or car.

Cities

Poland has many cities. Kraków, Łódź and Wrocław are the biggest cities after Warsaw. I live in Kraków, in the south of Poland.

Kraków and Wrocław

Kraków and Wrocław are two of Poland's most beautiful cities. Kraków is an old walled city with a **medieval** castle. Wrocław in western Poland is famous for its bridges – there are over a hundred of them! There is also a big zoo.

The Oder river in Wrocław

City centres

Many cities have a central square edged with brightly painted buildings. On market days squares are packed with stalls selling food, clothes and jewellery.

Biggest cities

Warsaw: 1,700,000 people
Łódź: 769,000
Kraków: 755,000
Wrocław: 635,000

Christmas market, Kraków

North and south

Gdánsk is a busy northern **port** on the Baltic Sea. It is famous for ship-building. The southern city of Katowice lies in Poland's biggest coal **mining** area. Mining is an important industry in Poland. Copper and silver are also mined in Poland.

Countryside and wildlife

I live in the countryside in northern Poland.

Good to grow

The fields here in the countryside are very **fertile**. The main crops are rye, wheat, potatoes, sugar beet and cabbages.

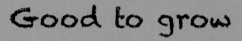

Coast and lakes

The Baltic coast has long, sandy beaches with sand dunes. Masuria in northeast Poland is known as the 'land of a thousand lakes'. Waterbirds arrive in spring to lay eggs and raise their young.

Leba Beach, Baltic coast

chamois

Mountains

The Carpathian Mountains lie on the border with Slovakia. They include the Tatras, Poland's highest mountains. Some peaks are covered with snow all year round. Wolves and deer-like animals called chamois live in the mountains.

Forest animals

Forests all over Poland are home to shy animals that are rare in Europe. There are brown bears, wild boars and large deer called elk. Wild cats called lynx hunt rabbits and deer.

lynx

What we eat

Food in Poland is filling, so there's no need to go hungry!

Polish dishes

Traditional Polish cooking is often rich and hearty, using plenty of cream and eggs. Soups, stews, stuffed dumplings and pancakes are all popular.

Eating meat

Meat dishes are popular in Poland. Farmers rear cattle, pigs and **poultry** for beef, pork, ham and chicken. Polish people like sausages – hundreds of different types are sold in shops and markets!

sausages

borscht

What's for supper?

Most families eat their main meal in the evening. It often starts with soup, made from beetroot, cabbage or mushrooms. Beetroot soup is called *borscht*. The main course could be a spicy stew called *bigos*, made with meat and cabbage. Cakes, pancakes, pastries and ice cream are tasty desserts.

Stuffed dumplings

Pierogi are a traditional Polish dish. These are small dumplings filled with meat, potatoes, mushrooms, cheese or fruit. You spoon the filling into a little circle of dough, fold it over and then boil for a few minutes — delicious!

Having fun

There's lots to do outdoors in Poland! We also like watching sport and making crafts.

Getting active

Walking, cycling and camping are our favourite ways of relaxing. You can do these in the mountains, in a forest or by a lake.

Mountain fun

In summer people visit the mountains to go walking, biking, climbing and fishing. In winter you can go skiing or tobogganing.

Seaside and lakes

In summer Poles head for the seaside. Here you can swim, sail or look for amber (see box). If the sea is too far away, you can swim, canoe or windsurf on a river or a lake!

Amber

Amber is a shiny orange material found on Baltic beaches. It is used to make jewellery.

Sport

Football is the most popular sport in Poland. Poles also enjoy watching and playing basketball, tennis and athletics.

At home

On rainy days paper cutting or *wycinanki* → is a traditional pastime. Paper cuts of flowers and animals decorate walls and furniture in Polish houses.

Famous places and people

Poland has many amazing places to visit. Our country is famous for palaces and castles, a reminder of the days when Poland was ruled by kings.

Castle

Malbork Castle is one of the biggest castles in Europe. It was first built in the 13th century, but has been added to over many years. It lies on the River Nogat in northern Poland.

Salt mines

Wieliczka Salt Mine in southern Poland is like an underground city. Salt has been mined here since the 13th century. There are tunnels, a lake and even a chapel with statues carved from salt.

The chapel in Wieliczka Salt Mine

Bison

National parks protect Poland's scenery and wildlife. In Białowieża Forest you can see bison. These large, shaggy beasts stand nearly two metres tall and can weigh a tonne!

Statues and memorials

Cities have statues of famous Poles. Nicolas Copernicus was an **astronomer**. He was the first person to say the Earth moved around the Sun, not the other way around. Scientist Marie Curie and **composer** Frédéric Chopin were other famous Poles. There are also many **memorials** to the Polish Jews who died in the Second World War.

Festivals and special days

The most important Polish festivals are Easter and Christmas. Other festivals held only in Poland mark the different seasons.

Christmas and Easter

People eat special foods at Christmas and Easter. They eat jam doughnuts to mark the start of **Lent**, the four weeks before Easter. At Easter they give brightly coloured eggs. There are water fights on Easter Monday! On Christmas Eve, families often gather for a special meal and presents before going to church.

Easter eggs

Music and dance

Folk festivals are held in summer. People dress in traditional costume and perform Polish dances such as the *mazurka*. Folk music is popular, but there are also big rock and pop concerts!

Marking the seasons

Special Polish festivals celebrate the seasons. Drowning Marzanna is a spring custom. People throw dolls that represent winter into the river to show winter is over. At Wianki festival in summer people float flowers and candles on water. The Feast of Greenery is a harvest festival.

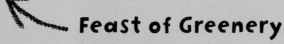

Feast of Greenery

Poland: Fast facts

Capital: Warsaw

Population: 38.5 million (2013)

Area: 312,679 sq km

Languages: Polish

Currency: The zloty

Main religions: Roman Catholicism

Longest river: Vistula 1,047 km

Highest mountain: Rysy, 2,503 m

National holidays: New Year's Day (1 January), Epiphany (6 January), Easter, Easter Monday, Labour Day (1 May), Constitution Day (3 May), Assumption Day / Polish Armed Forces Day (15 August), All Saints' Day (1 November), Independence Day (11 November), Christmas Day, Boxing Day (26 December)

Glossary

astronomer a scientist who studies planets and stars

border a line that divides two countries

capital city where the country's government meets

composer a person who writes music

descended from to be related to someone who lived long ago

fertile good for growing crops

folk traditional to the people who live in a place

Lent a special time in the Christian Church that covers the forty days that run up to Easter

mass a Christian church service

medieval dating back to the 11th to 14th centuries

memorial a statue or reminder of something that happened in the past

mining to dig natural materials, such as salt, from the ground

parliament a country's government

plain an area of low, flat land

Pope the leader of the Roman Catholic Church

port a place by the sea from where ships arrive and depart

poultry chickens

Slavs the people that are descended from a group of people that originally lived in central and eastern Europe, and speak Slavic languages

thatched a roof made of reeds or straw

traditional something that has been done in the same way for many years

Index